A Note to Parents

Dorling Kindersley Readers is a compelling new program for beginning readers, designed in conjunction with leading literacy experts, including Dr. Linda Gambrell, President of the National Reading Conference and past board member of the International Reading Association.

Beautiful illustrations and superb full-color photographs combine with engaging, easy-to-read stories to offer a fresh approach to each subject in the series. Each *Dorling Kindersley Reader* is guaranteed to capture a child's interest while developing his or her reading skills, general knowledge, and love of reading.

The four levels of *Dorling Kindersley Readers* are aimed at different reading abilities, enabling you to choose the books that are exactly right for your child:

Level 1 – Beginning to read
Level 2 – Beginning to read alone
Level 3 – Reading alone
Level 4 – Proficient readers

The "normal" age at which a child begins to read can be anywhere from three to eight years old, so these levels are intended only as a general guideline.

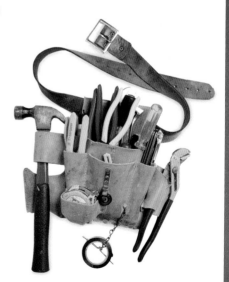

No matter which level you select, you can be sure that you are helping your child learn to read, then read to learn!

Dorling **DK** Kindersley

LONDON, NEW YORK, SYDNEY, DELHI, PARIS,
MUNICH, and JOHANNESBURG

A DORLING KINDERSLEY BOOK
www.dk.com

Produced by Southern Lights
Custom Publishing

For Dorling Kindersley
Publisher Andrew Berkhut
Executive Editor Andrea Curley
Art Director Tina Vaughan
Photographer Keith Harrelson

Reading Consultant
Linda Gambrell, Ph.D.

First American Edition, 2001
00 01 02 03 04 05 10 9 8 7 6 5 4 3 2 1
Published in the United States by
Dorling Kindersley Publishing, Inc.
95 Madison Avenue, New York, New York 10016

Published in Great Britain by Dorling Kindersley Limited.

Library of Congress Cataloging-in-Publication Data

Hayward, Linda
    A day in the life of a builder / by Linda Hayward. -
1st American ed.
    p. cm. -- (Dorling Kindersley readers)
    Audience:"Level 1, preschool-grade 1."
    ISBN 0-7894-7364-X   ISBN 0-7894-7363-1 (pbk.)
    1. Building--Juvenile literature. 2.House construction-Juvenile
literature.[1. House construction 2. Building. 3. Occupations.]
    I. Title. II. Series.

TH149 .H39 2001
690--dc21   00-055540

Printed and bound in China by L. Rex Printing Co., Ltd.

The characters and events in this story are fictional and do
not represent real persons or events. The author would like to
thank Michael Schuler for his help.

see our complete
catalog at
www.dk.com

DORLING KINDERSLEY *READERS*

BEGINNING

1

TO READ

A Day in the Life of a Builder

Written by Linda Hayward

A Dorling Kindersley Book

 6:45 a.m.

Jack and Sara Dale wake
their son, Steve. "I'm going to
work now," Jack says.

Today will be
a busy day.
Ten phone calls.
Five new houses.
One meeting.

Jack is a builder.

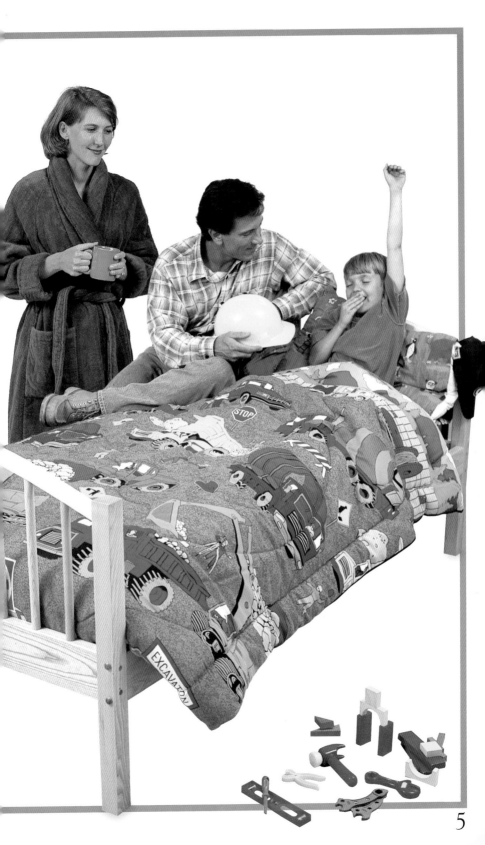

7:30 a.m.

At his office,
Jack plans his day.
He is in charge of
building five houses.

hard hat

Building a house takes many
workers. Jack puts on his hard
hat. Let's go see the houses and
how the workers are doing.

bulldozer

On Pine Street, Pete drives the bulldozer. He is clearing the land to build a house.

Jack brings Pete a jackhammer to break up the big rocks.

jackhammer

10:00 a.m.

Jack goes to check
the next house. Larry
is laying water pipes.

water
pipes

Here comes Bob.
"Do I pour this
concrete here?"
he asks.

"No! Follow me
to the Wilsons'
house," says Jack.

The Wilsons' house is almost finished. But it still needs a driveway. Bob's concrete mixer makes concrete.

concrete
mixer

Ted spreads
the concrete
for a smooth
driveway.

Oh, no!
Here come two dogs!

Will Ted have
to start all over again?
The Wilsons are
moving in next week!

12:00 p.m.

Jack visits
another house.

Bill needs help to
finish the frame.
Bill's helper is
sick today.

frame

17

Jack puts on his tool belt.

He helps Bill
finish the frame.
Jack hammers
in the last nail.

tool belt

2:00 p.m.

At the next house, George is working on the roof.

He hammers on the shingles to keep out the rain.

Don't miss a spot!

4:00 p.m.

Jack goes back to
the Wilsons' house.

Ted fixed the
driveway!

Inside, Carol works in the bathroom. She will use a drill to hang a towel bar.

drill

Here come the Wilsons. They are ready to see their new house.

They love it! Mrs. Wilson even says the driveway looks great.

Jack smiles.

Michael can't wait to see his new room. "My son has a hat just like yours," Jack says.

"I have a baseball and a bat, too!' says Michael.

Michael likes his room.
He knows just where to
put all his things. He waves
good-bye to Jack.

6:00 p.m.

The Dale family is happy
to be home.

"What's for dinner?"
Steve asks.

After dinner Jack makes
three phone calls.
He needs to find out about
the houses he is working on.

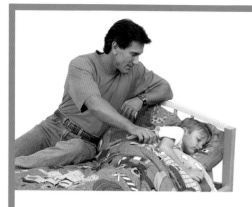

Jack says
good night
to Steve.

9:00 p.m.

Jack looks at Steve's hat.
He thinks about Michael
and his new room.

Jack smiles.
He has the
best job in
the world.

Picture Word List

hard hat

page 7

concrete
mixer

page 13

bulldozer

page 8

frame

page 16

jackhammer

page 8

tool belt

page 18

water
pipes

page 10

drill

page 23